About the Author

Linda Ward is a retired elementary school teacher who has been married to her husband and best friend since 1982.
They have three grown children, their spouses and five grandchildren. Her passion as a teacher was reading and teaching students to read.
Her first book, Jesus In The Manger, was published in 2017.
As a teacher in Texas, one of her favorite themes to teach was Texas history and explore the many environments, landscapes, wildlife and sheer vastness of the state. She moved from the deserts of West Texas to the North Texas area in 2019 to get closer to her children and grandchildren that live throughout Texas.
Linda's hobbies include Bible studies, cooking, gardening and being "Nana" to her precious grandkids and fur babies.

Linda Ward

I Spy
with my Boxer Eye

illustrated by László Veres & Penny Weber

I spy with my Boxer eyes,
Rocky Mountain ranges and desert basins,
Connected together under peaceful blue skies.
Delicate and exquisite are the scarce desert flowers;
The Yucca, the Barrel and Prickly Pear Cacti.

In my youthful romps in desert places
I chased rabbits, lizards, quail and doves.
Sometimes spring rains gave the perfect graces;
For the hidden poppies to magically appear
Creating a carpet of fanciful dancing yellow faces.

Careful observers can hear animal duets
Of coyotes and hawks in the cool desert nights.
While mountains change colors in majestic sunsets;
Brown, green and grey become orange, blue and purple
Creating a spectacular canvas one never forgets.

I spy with my Boxer eyes,
Palo Duro Canyon in the Texas Panhandle.
The landscape is changing where the Eastern sun rises;
Leaving canyons cut deep for great plains and tall grasses,
Where oil jacks and windmills display manmade devices.

Continuing South and some to the East,
Again the land changes into the Texas Hill Country.
Armadillos, raccoons and deer are just a few of the beasts;
Making homes in the Live Oak and Pecan trees protection,
Look closely for Bluejays and Cardinals, for a colorful feast.

Spring paints these Hills with Bluebonnets and Wildflowers,
While Mockingbirds sing songs they can mimic from others;
Like insects, amphibians and other birds, while singing for hours.
This is also the place where the Alamo still stands,
An unmistakable landmark against the sky where it towers.

I spy with my Boxer nose,
Distinctive smells of the Coastal Wetlands.
With beaches, tide pools and sand in my toes;
Returning back here to the place I was born
Where the sun rises early and the wind always blows.

The coastlines are rich with plants, animals and shells;
Where land meets the sea, white waves will greet you.
On beaches where Crabs, Pelicans and Seagulls dwell;
Sea Turtles will migrate to their breeding beds,
Laying eggs in the sand driven by instinct and smells.

A fisherman's paradise is this salty sea air;
Playful Dolphins ride waves and Sharks sneak about,
Making fish stories more interesting for all those who share.
Hours of sunlight, endless beaches with friends
The largest Gulf playground just about anywhere.

I spy with my Boxer ears,

From the Coast going North to Blackland Prairies and Lakes

I now roam through rich woodlands, it gives me such cheers.

Growing up in the desert, I thought that was hot;

But these lakes, rivers, streams provide humidity that seers.

In my North Texas home my senses have found
Squirrels chirping and taunting me and rabbits make chases,
Where Pecan, Oak and Maple trees cover the ground.
Crape Myrtles bloom everywhere and so do the flowers.
God's spectacular gardens make me one happy hound.

Texas regions are vast and I did my best,
To share landscapes and regions of this magnificent state.
Truly there's no place quite like it from the East to the West.
Go explore if you will Mountains, Lakes, Prairies and Plains
The Hill Country, Woodlands, and Gulf Coast, you will surely be blessed!

About the Illustrators

Laszlo Veres has been a professional illustrator for 30 years.
He uses computer technology, mainly various 3D software applications,
to make his very detailed, life-like illustrations.
He resides in Hungary.

Penny Weber is an illustrator from Long Island, New York.
She draws and paints her pictures digitally using Adobe Photoshop.
Penny lives with her husband, three children
and their very fat cat Tiger.

www.ingramcontent.com/pod-product-compliance
Lightning Source LLC
Chambersburg PA
CBRC101827090426
42811CB00023B/1916

A Child's Guide to Basic Birds

by

Terry Gene Doman Gibbon

Introduction

Based on the premise that young children are apt to appreciate those things with which they have personal contact, this book is designed to help instill a fundamental appreciation of nature and, in turn, of all life at an early age. Its bold, colorful illustrations and clever verses introduce the child to the most easily observed animal kingdom ~ The Birds.

A Child's Guide to Basic Birds is geared toward young children who are being exposed to the world of birds for the first time. It presents 30 of the most basic birds in two carefully planned groups, so that it "grows" with the child's curiosity and ability. Simple tips on attracting birds are provided, which can help a youngster's interest evolve into a true hobby.

It should be noted that, while *A Child's Guide to Basic Birds* attempts to present common birds in groups most likely to be observed together by the young child (or backyard bird watcher), the birds of a neighborhood are not obligated to appear in your yard in *printed order!* Therefore, a child who lives in an area surrounded by fields, for example is sure to spot the Barn Swallow or the Killdeer of Group 2, before the Downy and Hairy Woodpeckers presented in Group 1. Furthermore, this book is intended to be the *child's* guide to *basic* birds, not the *only* guide! It is recommended that parents obtain a complete guide for the family library, so that they can help the child identify the less common birds that will occasionally visit his feeder.

How to Use This Book

Designed to grow with children, **A Child's Guide to Basic Birds** meets the needs of children from about age 4 to 7. To the pre-schooler it offers colorful pictures and simple rhymes which he will enjoy as his parents read the book to him. As he becomes familiar with the entire book, his knowledge is gradually expanded from the general term "birdie" to the point where he is able to actually identify 33 different kinds of birds. Depending on his age and enthusiasm, he may learn these over a period of a few months or a couple of years.

While it is not necessary to utilize the book in any way beyond the function of the normal picture/nursery rhyme book, the learning experience can be greatly enhanced by setting up a bird feeding program which will suddenly add the fascinating element of *life* to each picture and verse. Each of the groups of birds presented is, therefore, followed by tips and projects which can turn the simple picture book into an educational hobby.

Looking more closely at the format of the book, it should be noted that **A Child's Guide to Basic Birds** is not only divided into two groups of birds, but also that the presentation of each bird consists of three elements. The most important of these is the picture, because simple recognition of different kinds of birds is the first step for the young child, a step which does not even require the ability to read. The second element is the verse. Printed in large type for the young reader, each presents factual information about the bird in rhyme so that it is easily retained. The third element consists of more detailed information which will become increasingly important as the child grows and is capable of mastering more facts about each of the birds he has learned to identify.

When the child had become thoroughly familiar with the birds introduced in this book, he will probably be ready to handle the information and formats of several of the adult guides currently on the market. These books vary greatly in their detail and should be carefully reviewed for their suitability.

Starting Out

A backyard bird feeding program can be as elaborate as one wishes to make it. In planning one for a young child, however, a simple arrangement can be as effective as the most intricate one. The key to success is to set up a feeder where the child can observe birds at close range. Bring the bird up to the window, for example, and that gray spot suddenly takes on personality; the word, "Chickadee" takes on real meaning.

There are all sorts of different kinds of feeders on the market these days. Some are designed to accommodate certain types of birds or only small-sized birds, providing small holes through which to get the seed, or little perching surface, etc. There are even some these days that are very effective at deterring squirrels - which can certainly be good, as you can have so many that the birds don't actually get much chance to use your feeder! ~ Squirrels can be fun and entertaining to watch, too, however, and beautiful birds come in all sizes, so you may wish to provide one or more feeders which can accommodate the larger birds (and even the squirrels!)

In the pages at the end of each of the two sections of birds, you will find some simple instructions for making simple bird feeders and bird houses, which you can make at home and set-up to help attract birds to your yard.

There're many different kinds of birds,
      As you will quickly see;
Like Robins, Killdeer, Grackles and
      The Black-capped Chickadee.

The Cardinal, Blue Jay, and Titmouse
      Each has a crested head;
But jays are blue and titmice gray and
      Cardinals are bright red.

The tiny little hummingbird
      Has a straw-like beak;
And great big crows are very smart,
      A few have learned to "speak"!

Now, if you live nearby a woods
　　Woodpeckers may come out;
But if you live in open fields,
　　Then swallows fly about!

So now you know that "bird"'s a word
　　That holds much more to learn.
You'll find another kind of bird
　　With each page that you turn . . . . .

The Robin

A common bird with orange-red breast
The Robin brings the Spring.
With mud and grass he'll build his nest,
And all the while he'll sing.

The eggs may number three to five
And are a bright, bright blue;
He feeds the babies wiggly worms
And big black beetles, too!

Length: 8 ½ inches
Female: Similar to male, but paler in coloring.
Immature: Streaked breast.
Voice: A string of clearly whistled phrases of 3 to 4 notes each.

Found throughout the country at given times of the year, including in the suburbs.
Feeds on the ground, in grass, backyards, and orchard land.
Builds nest on horizontal surfaces; will use nesting shelves
provided by bird-loving people.

The Cardinal

A well known bird who is bright red
The Cardinal's face is black.
He has a crest upon his head
And *dark red* on his back.

The female's tan instead of red,
But it's clear what she is.
Her bright orange beak & crested head
Will prove that she is his!

They're attracted by the sunflower
And love to eat its seed;
So if you keep your feeder filled
These birds will come to feed.

Length: 7 ¾ inches.
Female: Tan with red-orange coloring on wings and tail feathers
and on tip of the crest. Thick, conical beak,
like that of the male.
Voice: Song is made up of long clear whistles,
slurred together; loud and distinctive.

Found primarily in the eastern half of the country;
also in the Southwest. Common in suburbs,
hedgerows, and wooded borders.
A regular visitor to bird feeders, in many cities, as well as
in rural areas. At feeders, the male often seems to stand aside
and observe more than he feeds!

The Blue Jay

The Blue Jay is a noisy bird
Of several shades of blue.
His common call may well be heard
In woods and city, too!

He's not afraid to guard his nest
From large and hungry cats.
He dives down bravely at the pest
~ He's noted for such spats!

Length: 10 inches.
Female: Similar to male; paler.
Voice: Most commonly galls a distinct "jay, jay", in pairs.
High pitched when compared to the "caw" of
the common crow. Sings other notes, some musical in nature.

Found throughout the eastern two-thirds of the country,
often remaining north in the winter months. Some migration,
however, from the extreme northern limits of its range.
A frequent visitor to bird feeders, inclined to
bully smaller birds at times.

The Mockingbird

The Mockingbird sings out the songs
Of lots of other birds;
He mimics their calls all day long
~ The best you've ever heard!

He sometimes likes to sing at night
Much like the Nightingale.
And when he flies he flashes white
That's on his wings and tail.

Length: 9 inches.
Female: Like the male.
Voice: Mimics the calls and songs of other birds,
repeating each six times or more before
switching to another. Repertoire will vary
with the birds found in its neighborhood.
Also calls a sharp "tchack".

Common throughout southern regions of the country,
ranging farther north in the East than in the West.
Populates suburbs, rural regions, and city edges.
Often seen singing, perched high in a tree or on
a rooftop. A common visitor to bird feeders and
backyards generally.

The Starling

The Starling has a lot of color
   For a bird who's black.
But in the winter he's much duller,
   With spots on breast and back.

He's often thought of as a pest
   As where there's one, there're thirty!
His looks and habits are, at best,
   Sloppy and quite dirty!

Length: 6 to 8 ½ inches.
Winter: Dull black or brown with light speckles
liberally sprinkled on it; dark bill which
gradually turns yellow as Spring approaches.
Voice: Many harsh and raucous notes. Also an
impressive mimic, reproducing songs
very pleasant to the ears!

Found throughout the country; common in cities,
parks, and farmlands. In backyards
and at bird feeders Starlings will often be far
too numerous to be enjoyed!

The House Sparrow

The first time that you see this one
You might be quite excited;
But you may find you're over-run
With Sparrows not invited!

The House Sparrow can be a pest,
Although he is quite pretty.
He takes to feeders with great zest
In rural land and city.

Length: 5 ¼ inches.
Female: Easily confused with other Sparrows.
Brown streaked back and plain buff
or dingy colored breast. Bold buff stripe
over eye is distinctive mark.
Immature: Resembling the female, with young males
gradually evolving to the appearance
of the adult male.
Voice: A string of uninteresting chirping notes.

Abundant throughout the country, farm and city alike;
often in flocks. City birds often seem much duller
than their country counterparts, because of soot!
Inclined to be pests at bird feeders, because of
their great numbers. Originally from Europe, they are
also known as the "English Sparrow".

The Chickadees

The little Black-capped Chickadee,
And others of his kind,
Will hang from branches upside-down
And never seem to mind.

He'll hop and play upon the snow
Or sit upon your hand.
This friendly little acrobat's
A favorite in the land!

There are a half dozen kinds of Chickadees found across the country. While each is distinctive, they are all *clearly Chickadees!* The Black-capped Chickadee and Carolina Chickadee are most easily confused, being very similar in appearance and having territories which over-lap in some eastern regions. The Black-capped is slightly larger, with rustier sides, whiter cheek patches, white feather edges on the wings, a lower and slower call and song, etc. The Black-cap's range is also more extensive than other Chickadees', and it covers a great portion of the North and northwestern continent not inhabited by the Carolina Chickadee. All Chickadees are friendly birds, visiting feeders loyally and making use of nesting boxes provided. Black-capped Chickadees are particularly easy to hand-tame.

Length: 4 ¼ to 4 ½ inches.
Females and immature look like the males.
Voice: All Chickadees call a variation of "chick-a-dee-dee-dee".

The Tufted Titmouse

The Titmouse is a crested bird
Who's smaller than a jay;
With a splash of orange on his sides,
He's mostly white and gray.

He loves to come to feeders
For seed and suet, too;
And he loves peanut butter
As little children do!

Length: 5 ½ inches.
Female: Like the male.
Immature: Similar to the adults, but less distinct markings and slightly brownish in color.
Voice: Usually two whistled notes, quite loud "peter-peter". Sometimes slurred, sounding like one note.

The Tufted Titmouse is common in the eastern half of the country, especially in deciduous woods and suburbs with wooded lots. Friendly and agile, the Titmouse is a regular visitor to bird feeders and will build its nest in bird-houses.

There are several kinds of Titmice found in the United States and Mexico, but the Tufted Titmouse is the most common. As with Chickadees, all the varieties are *clearly Titmice!*

The White-breasted Nuthatch

Not many birds hop *down* a tree
The way the Nuthatch can.
He'll cock his head way up to see
If he encounters man.

He hunts for bugs the whole day long
And has a special bill
That's long and thin and very strong
And helps him catch his fill!

Length: 5 inches.
Female: Similar to male, but with grayish cap,
instead of black.
Voice: A quiet "ank, ank".

Common in eastern and western regions, but not
found in a central strip of the country. Prefers deciduous
woodlands, and is common in suburbs with wooded acreage.
A regular visitor to bird feeders and will use nesting boxes.
Often found with the Black-capped Chickadee
and the Tufted Titmouse. As with the Chickadees and Titmice,
there are other varieties of Nuthatches in the country,
but the are all *clearly Nuthatches.*

The American Goldfinch

The Goldfinch is a yellow bird
With wings of black and white.
He sometimes flocks in weedy fields,
And makes the landscape bright.

He loves sunflower and thistle
Much more than other seeds;
He calls a long clear whistle
From trees near where he feeds.

Length: 4 ¼ to 5 ½ inches.
Female: Similar to the male, but not as bright,
with no black cap, and having an olive-yellow back.
Immature and male in winter resemble the female.
Voice: Song is canary-like, with notes that are long and clear.

Found in migration throughout the country, the American
Goldfinch is the "state bird" of some states. Prefers
weedy fields with seed bearing bushes and trees,
weeds such as dandelions, thistles, and sunflowers.
Often found along roadsides in the suburbs and in farmlands.
Will visit feeders readily, especially when filled
with sunflower or thistle (when purchased in feed stores,
it is actually the similar "niger seed" rather than thistle.)
at feed stores.)

The Downy Woodpecker and the Hairy Woodpecker

There are woodpeckers of all kinds
Which you won't often see,
But the Downy isn't hard to find
Pecking on a tree!

By loudly pecking holes in wood
He catches bugs for food;
And then the holes are very good
To nest and raise a brood.

The Hairy Woodpecker's much the same,
But bigger to behold.
Put suet in your bird feeder
And both birds may be bold!

The Downy Woodpecker (pictured here)

Length: Averages 6 to 7 inches
Female: Similar to male; lacking red head patch.
Voice: Calls a flat sounding "pic". A so rapid succession of notes, with pitch descending at the end.

The Hairy Woodpecker

8 ½ to 10 ½ inches.
Similar to male; lacking red head patch.
A sharp "peek", louder than Downy's note. Also a Kingfisher-like rattle run together more than the Downy's.

Downy and Hairy Woodpeckers are found year round throughout the country; Hairy's range extends farther south and north than the Downy's. Both favor mixed or deciduous woods, but the Downy also ventures into orchards, suburbs, and backyard shade trees. Very similar in appearance, they are most readily distinguished by the difference in size. Hairy also has a much larger and longer bill, proportionately, than the Downy. Both birds can be attracted to suet feeders and will also use nesting boxes. The Downy will occasionally visit a feeder filled only with seed.

The Red-headed Woodpecker

A bird that you should certainly know,
But you may never see,
This woodpecker is much more rare
Than he once used to be.

He likes the open leafy wood;
He'll perch there in plain sight.
His field marks are his bright red hood
And wing patch of pure white.

Length: 7 ½ to 9 ½ inches.
Female: Like the male.
Immature: Streaked or dusky brown. White wing patch
is distinctive, as it is in the adult.
Voice: Calls a loud "quer-r-k".

Found throughout the eastern United States year round and farther west
and north in the summer, but is uncommon in much of its range.
Prefers open deciduous woods, enjoying wooded parks and gardens.
Also found in open coniferous forests. Pecks cavity in tree or pole,
8 to 80 feet from the ground, in which to build its nest.

The Turkey Vulture

Sometimes you'll see a giant bird
Soaring through the sky,
Whose wings are held to form a "V"
You can identify.

The Turkey Vulture can be seen
Circling all year round.
They're often spied in two's or more,
And *sometimes* on the ground.

Length: 25 to 30 inches.
Wing-span: as much as 72 inches.
Immature: Similar to adults, but with black head,
instead of red.

A common vulture throughout the country, except northern
New England and parts of the Great Lakes region.
Usually seen soaring in large circles, shifting its weight from side to side.
In flight the winds are held in a broad V-shape.
From below the wings are visibly two-toned, having lighter flight feathers
than the fore part of the wing. Turkey Vultures feed on carrion
in the fields and along roadsides. If desired, they can sometimes
be attracted to feeders where raw, red meat is offered.

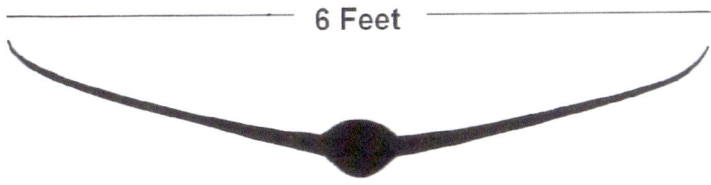

6 Feet

The Mallard Duck

A common duck in parks and ponds,
The Mallard's often tame.
The children throw them bread to eat,
While hunters call them "game".

The males have heads of shiny green,
Their necks are ringed with white;
With orange webbed feet & yellow bills
That don't hurt when they bite!

Length: 16 inches.
Wing-span: 36 inches.
Female: Mottled brown. Blue wing feather and
lighter color distinguish it from the Black Duck.
Voice: A classic "quack", sometimes amusingly
loud and definite.

Found in migration across most of the continent, in ponds
and fresh water marshes. Semi-domesticated Mallards in parks
and backyard ponds often do not migrate. Surface feeders,
they dunk their heads under water, and with their tails in the air,
they gather vegetation from the bottom of ponds. They also eat small fish,
mollusks, insects, and seeds of grasses and weeds.
The Mallard's "quack" is the noise people associate with ducks.

The Ring-necked Pheasant

The Pheasant is a thrill to see,
If you have them around;
He roams through tall and weedy fields
And feeds upon the ground.

He'll wander into your back lawn
If grass near-by is tall,
You'll often hear, at dusk or dawn,
His loud and squawking call!

Length: 33 - 36 inches.
Female: 20 ½ inches; mottled brown with long,
pointed tail and short rounded wings.
Voice: A loud two syllabled squawk, often followed
by a whir of rapidly beating wings.

Introduced into the United States from China, the Ring-necked Pheasant
is found across the country, primarily north of the Mason-Dixon Line, at altitudes
where deep snow is not prohibitive, and into Canada, to the deep snow line of the North.
Most common in farmland brush, fields of corn and other grain, the Pheasant
is far less common in 2009 than it was when this book was first written, in 1976!
It is also found in open woods and hedgerows, and seen along roadsides,
ducking for cover. It roosts in trees, but feeds on the ground. It eats berries
and can be attracted to feeders where grain and seed are scattered on the ground.
It is also a target of hunters everywhere.

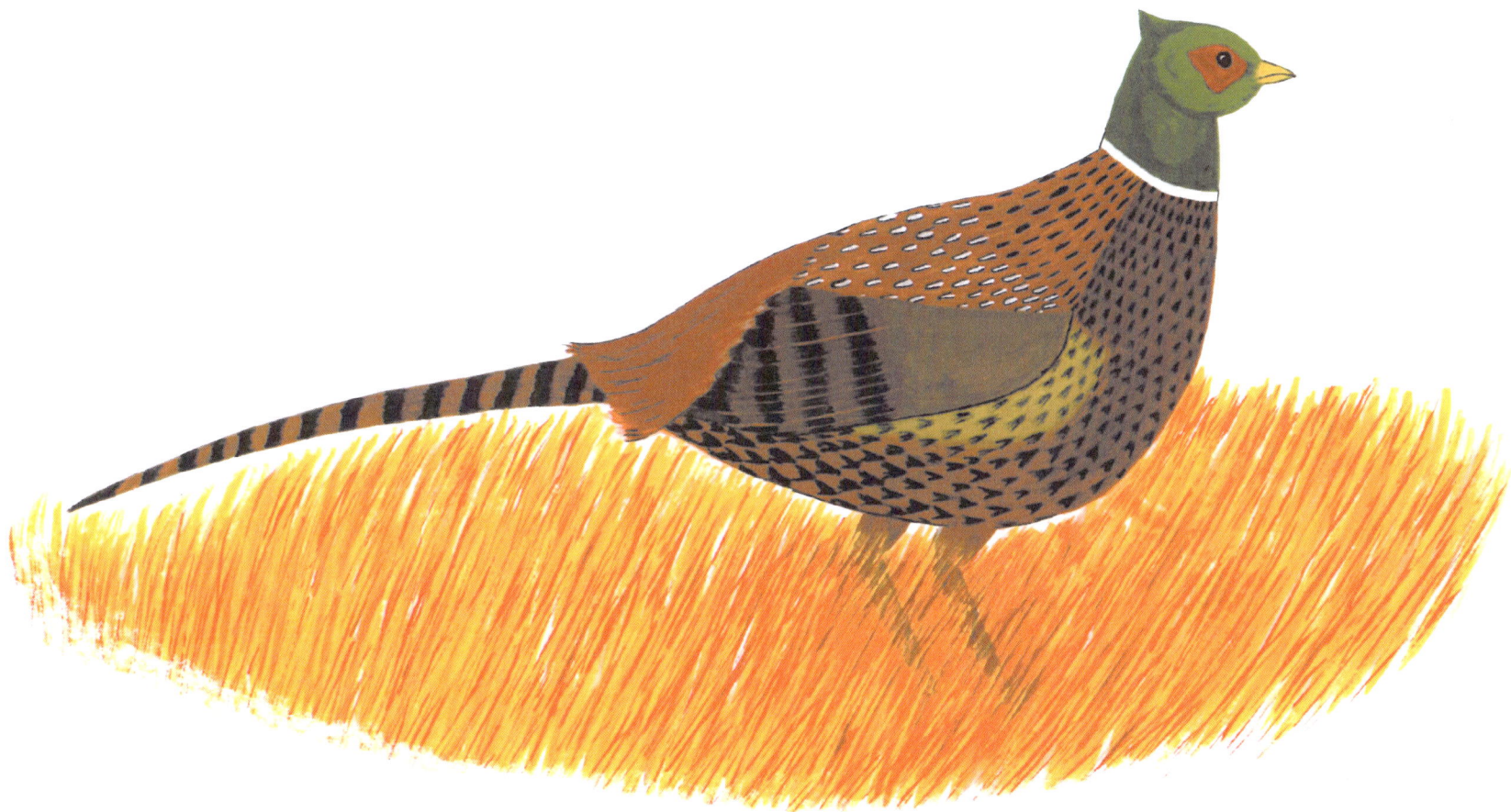

Red-winged Blackbird

Although birds are wild creatures, you can get many of them to come into your yard where you can watch them close up. One way to do this is to put up a bird feeder. In the Wintertime, feeding the birds helps them to live through the cold months when food is scarce. In the Springtime, you will be able to watch whole families of birds at your feeders.

Many different types of bird feeders can be purchased at feed stores and hardware stores, which can be hung from trees, put on posts, or even "suction-cupped" to a window. You can also make the feeder pictured above to fit right outside your bedroom window. It is made of wood scraps, so if you have never made things of wood and nails before, be sure to get your father or mother to help you.

1. Start with a flat board about 12 inches long and 8 or 10 inches wide, and nail four wooden sides onto it, that stick up high enough to keep the seed from falling out easily. If the sides don't fit exactly and are a little bit short, don't worry - small gaps at the corners will allow rain water to drain out more easily than it would otherwise.

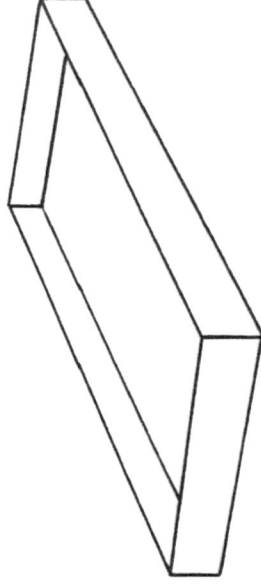

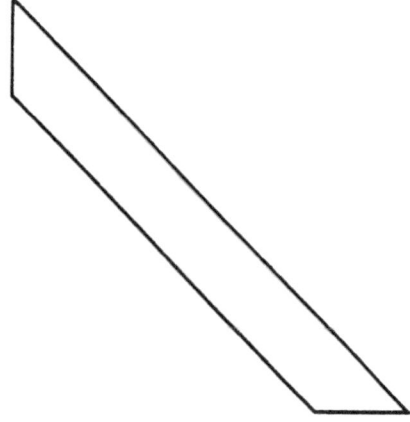

2. Next, make a brace to keep the feeder from drooping when it is put up. Use a stick of wood about 12 inches long and cut the ends off at an angle, as in the picture to the left.

3. Nail one end of the brace to the bottom of the feeder so that the end of it does *not line up with the back edge of the feeder.* (See below.)

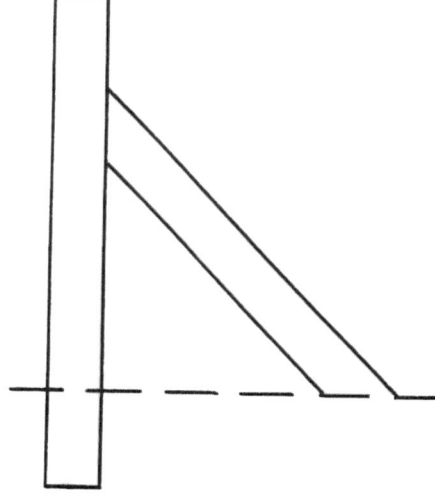

4. You are now ready to put up your bird feeder. Nail the back edge of the feeder shelf onto your windowsill, so that the brace touches the wall; then nail the brace to the wall.

Fill your bird feeder with a mixture or seen and forget about it until the birds discover that it is there. If you have a lot of trees around your house, they may find it within minutes; but if you do not, it could take them a couple of weeks!

Once the birds have found you bird feeder, you may want to put out suet and peanut- butter for them. The suet should be placed in a cage so that the bigger birds can't carry it off all at one time. The cage can be made easily with open mesh screen or from a nylon fruit bag. It can be added to the bird feeder you already have, but it is often better to make a separate feeder. You can purchase suet scraps at your grocery store. These days you can purchase reasonably priced wire feeders which hold specially made "suet cakes" at your feed or wild bird store, too. These store-bought suet cakes come in a variety of "flavors" which appeal to different types of birds. Many of them are also made to resist melting or otherwise going bad as they are subjected to the elements.

Wire suet feeder

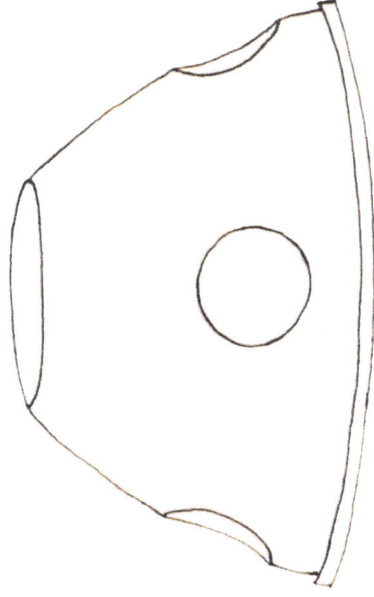

Peanut butter should be mixed with seed to keep the birds from choking on it. You can put a spoonful in a corner of your window feeder. You will find that squirrels and Starlings love this treat as much as Chickadees and Titmice do, so you may want to add a cover for the peanut butter, if you are bothered by them. The cover can be made from a plastic margarine dish. Just cut small holes in 3 or 4 sides of the dish, glue the lid upside-down securely onto the feeder shelf, and snap the dish into place on the lid with the peanut butter inside. The tighter the lid fits on the dish, the better it will work, especially against the clever squirrels! It won't keep either the squirrels or the Starlings out completely, but will help and will make it less likely that the Starlings to throw the peanut butter all over your window!

The Common Crow

A big black bird who can learn tricks,
The Crow is very smart.
A few have even learned to talk
Or play a movie part!

He likes to steal the planted seeds
From farmers' fields all day;
So farmers put up "scare-crow" men
To frighten him away!

Length: 17 inches.
Female: Similar to male.
Voice: Calls a distinctive "caw", often in pairs and more.

Found throughout the country, and is a year round resident
of most of the nation, except in extremely dry regions.
In flight, he can be confused with the Red-shouldered hawk,
but glides only seconds at a time. The Crow is not inclined to
visit bird feeders, per se, but is a common visitor to backyards
and farmlands, especially in areas which
have recently been seeded.

The Common Grackle

The Common Grackle has a head
That reflects blue or green;
The way the sunlight shines on it
Determines which is seen.

He's bigger that a Starling,
Much smaller that a Crow;
His yellow eyes and long straight tail
Are field marks you should know!

Length: 10 - 12 inches.
Female: Similar to the male, but smaller in size.
Voice: A harsh loud note, "chack".

Found throughout the eastern two-thirds of the country,
he is abundant in open fields. Congregates with other "blackbirds",
but is larger than most. Can also be distinguished by his yellow eyes
and long, wedge-shaped tail. A regular visitor to bird feeders
and recently seeded lawns, the Common Grackle sometimes
gathers in sufficient numbers to be a pest.
Also known as the "Purple Grackle".

The Yellow-shafted Flicker

To spot a Flicker is a treat
Although they're not so rare.
His back of white will catch your eye
When he flies through the air.

Like all the other Woodpeckers,
The Flicker hunts for bugs,
And in a hole that he pecks out
He makes a nest that's snug.

Length: 10 ½ inches.

Female: Similar to male, but lacking the "mustache" seen on the cheek of the male.

Voice: Loud two syllabled "flicker", or abbreviated call, "flick!"

Found throughout the eastern United States, year round, and much of Canada in the summer. Prefers open woods, but often seen in backyards in wooded neighborhoods. Distinguished in flight by white back or yellow under-wing area. Although the two western Flickers (the Red-shafted and the less common Gilded Flicker) are colored differently, the patterns of their markings are similar and clearly distinguish them as Flickers.

Flickers can be attracted to feeding stations where suet is offered and will also use large nesting boxes.

The Mourning Dove

The Mourning Dove's related to
The common pigeon clan;
He coos and also bobs his head;
His body's plump and tan.

He's common in suburban yards,
And in the city, too;
But doves don't flock on buildings
Like messy pigeons do!

Length: 10 ½ inches.
Female: Similar to male.
Voice: A sad or eerie sounding "coo",
often in pairs ("coo, coo"), probably responsible
for his "Mourning" name.

Found throughout the country, year round except
where winters are extremely harsh. Common in suburbs
and farm regions; also found in cities and is a visitor to
backyard feeding stations on or near the ground.
Sometimes more aggressive than his name
and reputation might suggest.

The Barn Swallow

The Barn Swallow can catch a bug
While darting through the skies.
His tail is forked and can be seen
Both perched and when he flies.

He builds mud nests on ledges flat,
Like on a building frame.
He likes to build them inside barns;
That's how he got his name!

Length: 6 inches.
Female and immature: Similar to male, but paler
in coloring on breast and throat.
Voice: Constant tweetering, particularly in flight.

Extremely common in open farmland throughout the country
during the summer months. Builds mud nests, often in colonies,
on level surfaces of barns and other buildings,
preferring to build them inside. Will use nesting shelves readily.
Flocks with other swallows, but is the only one
with a deeply forked tail. Catches bugs while darting
and flitting through the sky. Often seen following lawn mowers,
seeming to dive at them; in fact, they are catching the bugs
stirred up by the machines.

The Ruby-throated Hummingbird

The Ruby-throated Hummingbird
Can hover in the air;
He flaps his wings so very fast,
You hardly know they're there!

He drinks from flowers with a beak
That looks much like a straw.
He seems to be as strange a bird
As anyone ever saw!

Length: 3 inches
Female and immature: Similar to the male,
but lacking the red throat.

The only hummingbird found in the eastern half
of the country (except for occasional visits to the
Gulf coast states by the Rufous Hummingbird.)
This tiny bird is common in gardens where he drinks
nectar from tubular flowers, preferring those with red
blossoms. Easily attracted to special feeders, made to hold a
sugar-water solution, they are noted for their agility in flight.
They are able to hover nearly motionlessly,
and even fly backwards with ease.

The Rose-breasted Grosbeak

Rose-breasted Grosbeaks can't be missed
If there are males around.
They have thick bills and rosy bibs
And make a loud "peek" sound.

The female, on the other hand,
Is nowhere near a cinch.
She's like a great big sparrow
Or female Purple Finch.

Length: 7 ¼ inches.
Female: Brown and white streaked; looks much like
an over-grown female sparrow or Purple Finch.
Voice: Song similar to the Robin's. Call is
a single sharp note, "peek!"

Primarily a northwestern resident, the Rose-breasted Grosbeak
is common in deciduous woods and is also found in
suburban areas and mature orchards. Like that of the Cardinal,
his beak is specially designed to crack the shells of large seeds.
Can be attracted to backyard feeders, particularly where
sunflower seeds are offered.

Three other varieties of Grosbeaks are found across the nation.
Each has unique markings, but all have the conical bill and
the over-all shape of the Rose-breasted Grosbeak.

The Eastern Bluebird

The Bluebird had been dying out
'Till people showed concern;
And since we kept our minds on it
His numbers have returned.

Because we put up bird houses
For them to build their nests,
They have a place to lay their eggs
Where they are safe from pests!

Length: 5 ½ to 7 inches.

Female and immature: Female is similar to male, but paler in coloring. Immature is grayish, with speckled breast with no orange-red color.

Both are identified by "hunched" posture, white ring under the eye, and blue coloring in wings and tail.

Voice: Song is soft and melodious, notes grouped 3 to 4 together.

Found throughout most of the East in open farmland, but not really common in some of its range. It is the only *blue* bird with a orange-red breast in the East. The Eastern Bluebird had suffered a great decline in its population in second half of the twentieth century, due in part, to loss of nesting cavities, because of man's land development. A campaign to erect suitable bird houses has helped to reverse their decline, and in 2009 it can certainly be said that their numbers have returned significantly.

The Song Sparrow

The Song Sparrow's a little bird
Whose song is nice to hear.
He lives in fields or by a woods
With bushes to hide near.

His throat is white; his face is striped,
There are streaks upon his breast,
With a dark spot in the middle
To tell him from the rest.

Length: 5 ½ inches.
Female: Similar to the male.
Juvenile: Similar to the male,
but with less streaking on breast.
Voice: Musical song of many notes and trills.

Common nationwide during winter months; year round
in northern half of the country. Prefers brushy areas, fields,
hedgerows, etc. Can be attracted to bird feeders, particularly
when snow covers natural food sources. Nests 0 to 12 feet
above the ground, but most often 1 to 3 feet. Will use
open nesting shelf when provided.

The Slate-colored Junco

He's often called the "snowbird",
Because he loves the snow.
The little gray and white Junco's
And easy bird to know.

He likes to hide beneath a bush,
And feed upon the ground;
And when he flies or flips his tail
White feathers will be found!

Length: 5 ¼ inches.
Female: Similar to the male, sometimes lighter gray in coloring.
Voice: Tweetering; musical trills, somewhat similar to that
of the Chipping Sparrow.

Also known as the "Dark-eyed Junco" and the "Northern Junco",
this bird is found throughout much of the country in the winter,
except in the extreme South. A favorite of bird lovers, the Junco
frequents bird feeders, where he sometimes aggressively chases
other little birds away. He can be seen hopping inconspicuously under
bushes in suburbs and city alike. The pale beak and white outer
tail feathers are diagnostic field marks.

The "Oregon Junco" and the "White-winged Junco" are very similar,
but both have smaller ranges.

The Catbird

Related to the Mockingbird,
The Catbird is dark gray.
Although his cousin has more calls,
This bird has lots to say!

He'll tilt his tail so you can see
A patch of rusty red;
And 'though he's gray, he always wears
A black cap on his head!

Length: 8 to 9 inches.
Female: Similar to the male.
Voice: Catlike mew, squeaky and distinctive. Song is disjointed,
rarely repetitious. Mimics other birds, but not as
well as the Mockingbird does.

The Catbird is a Summer resident across the nation,
except in the far West and parts of the Southwest.
Resides near thickets, preferring dense cover.   Occasionally
visits bird feeders, but he is more often seen in trees and
brush nearby. The only dark gray bird with a black cap and rusty
color under tail coverts. His long tail, which he flicks,
is also a field mark.

The Rufous-sided Towhee

The Towhee's sides are trimmed with rust,
His body's black and white.
He'll often visit bird feeders,
And is a welcome sight.

The female looks about the same,
(Instead of black she's brown).
When they hop their tails flash white
While flipping up and down.

Length: 7 ¼ inches.
Female: Similar to male, but brown where the male is black.
Voice: A three note song, with the last note being drawn out
and higher in pitch than the others.

Common throughout the country year round, except
in the central states where it resides only during the winter months.
Prefers brushy areas and wooded margins. Popular visitor to
feeding stations in suburban regions. Western birds have additional
white spots on back and wings.   Southern variety may have white
or orange eye (iris). In all regions, the white tail feathers flash
distinctively as he hops through the brush.

The Killdeer

Much like the common sandpipers,
The Killdeer's legs are long;
He looks as if when he was built
The legs he got were wrong!

He likes to live in open fields,
Instead of by the sea.
He's known to lead you from the nest
By faking injury!

Length: 8 to 10 inches.
Female and immature: Similar to the male;
immature has only one neck band.
Voice: Repeats name; calls loudly in flight,
particularly near dusk.

Common throughout the country, residing in open fields
and farmland, not necessarily near water. Overall shape and walk,
long legs and neck bands are distinctive field marks. In flight, rusty
rump and black and white striped wing pattern are diagnostic.
Nests on the ground; known for feigning injury
to distract intruders away from the nest.

The Herring Gull

Of common birds along the shore
One is the Herring Gull.
While full grown birds are white and gray
The young are brown and dull.

These scavengers catch a lot of fish
And swimmers feed them, too;
If you toss bread for them to eat
These gulls will flock to you!

Length: 20 inches.
Female: Similar to the male.
Immature: First-winter birds are mottled brown; second-winter
birds are whiter with dark tail feathers and white rump.
Voice: Loud single notes, often "whining".

Winters along all coasts and major rivers of the country
and can be seen almost anywhere in migration. This very
common gull is primarily a scavenger, frequenting garbage dumps
as well as fishing ports and public beaches. Often seen soaring above
beaches and being fed by swimmers. In 2009, it is not uncommon to see
stray Herring Gulls in parking lots of coastal states,
far from the water of the shore.

The Canada Goose

Canada Geese are very large
And they will catch your eye.
Flocks migrate South in wintertime,
In V-shaped squads, they fly.

They're really not too friendly,
'Though some may come quite near;
But if you use your common sense
There is no need to fear.

Length: 24 to 35 inches.
Female: Similar to the male.
Voice: Double syllabled honking, characteristic in flight. Also "hisses" a warning.

Spends summer months in Canada, Alaska, and northern United States;
winters in southern coastal and central U.S. and even into Mexico.
Can be seen in migration across the entire country. The Canada Goose
is the most common goose on the North American continent. Its large size,
long black neck, and white cheek patch are diagnostic field marks.
There are many sub-species, varying in size and coloring.

The Canada Goose is a popular target of hunters.
In 2009, there numbers are great enough to be a problem,
to auto and airplane traffic. Where they gather in great numbers,
their excrement can be a big problem for people walking in parks and
yards. Some people even refer to them as, "rats with wings".

In the Springtime, you can attract birds into your yard by giving them a good place to raise their families. While trees and bushes provide natural nesting sites, cover, and food, many birds will also use man-made bird houses and nesting shelves. Putting these up will make it easier for you to find nests, and the birds who use nesting shelves will be quite easy to watch as the family grows up.

Like bird feeders, bird houses can be purchased in stores, but many kinds of birds won't like them, because birds can be very picky about the size of the nesting site and its entrance. Simple bird houses and shelves can be built for specific kinds of birds and instructions for both are given on the following pages, along with a chart telling what style and size nesting site to build for six different kinds of birds.

The basic bird house should have a floor, four walls (one of which has an entry hole for the birds to go in and out), and a roof which is hinged so that the house can be cleaned out at the end of the season.

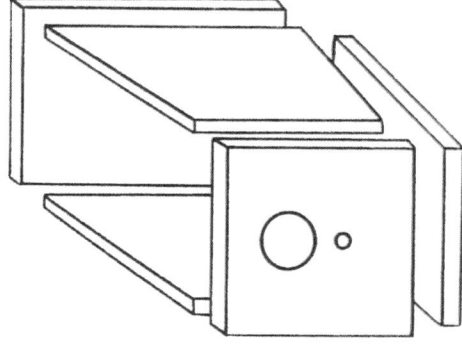

1. Referring to the chart for dimensions, begin by cutting out the floor board and other pieces. Then cut out the entry hole in the front wall and drill a few small drain holes in the floor. If you want to include a perch, drill a small hole under the entrance for a stick to go.

2. Put the house together: Using glue in the joints, nail the side walls to the floor, and nail the front and back walls to the floor and to the side walls. Hinge the roof to the top of the back wall so that it covers the top of the house and over-hangs a little bit. Place a perch in the hole under the entrance as in the picture at the left.

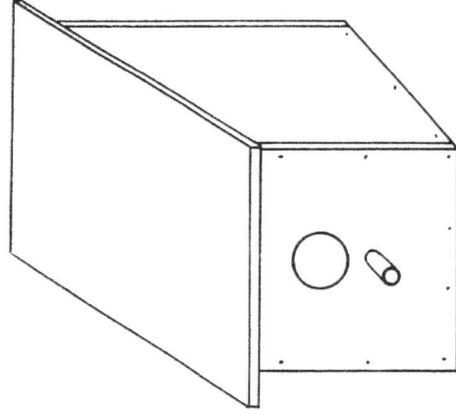

3. Finally, stain the house with a dark color so that it will not stand out when it is hung up. Wait for it to dry completely.

A nesting shelf is a bird house with one or more of the walls missing (and the roof is optional.) Check the chart to see how big the shelf should be and decide how many walls to put on it; then start building it just as you would build a complete bird house. Begin by cutting out the pieces and then put them together with nails and glue. Finally, stain the shelf a dark color and wait for it to dry.

When you have finished you bird house or nesting shelf you are ready to put it up.

Pick out a good spot which is sheltered from the weather and which cats and other enemies can not get at easily. Be sure you can hang it the right height from the ground (see chart), and get your father or mother to help you, since you will most likely need a ladder.

Once the house is hung up, keep an eye on it from a distance, but don't get too close, or the birds might not want to move in! If a bird couple does build a nest there, an *occasional* close-up peek won't hurt – but don't be a pest or you might scare the parents away!

	Floor	Height Back Wall	Height Front Wall	Entry Size	Height Entry From Floor	Distance From Ground (in feet)
Bluebird	5 x 5	8 - 10	8	1½	6	5 - 10
Chickadee	4 x 4	8 - 10	7 - 9	1⅛	6 - 8	6 - 15
Downy Woodpecker	4 x 4	8 - 10	7 - 9	1¼	6 - 8	6 - 20
House Wren	4 x 4	6 - 8	4 - 7	1	1 - 6	6 - 10
Robin	6 x 8	8	one to three walls			6 - 15
Barn Swallow	6 x 6	6				8 - 12

Note that all measurements in the chart above are in inches, except where indicated.

Kestrel
(also called the Sparrow Hawk)